Using the Commandments

Margaret Killingray

Lecturer, London Institute for Contemporary Christianity

Jo Bailey Wells

Dean, Clare College, Cambridge

GROVE BOOKS LIMITED
RIDLEY HALL RD CAMBRIDGE CB3 9HU

Contents

The Cover Illustration is by Peter Ashton

First Impression September 2000
ISSN 1365-490X
ISBN 1 85174 443 6

1

'For Our Lasting Good':
The Ten Commandments Today

My tongue will sing of your promise, for all your commandments are right.
Let your hand be ready to help me, for I have chosen your precepts.
I long for your salvation, O Lord, and your law is my delight.

Psalm 119's acrostic lyricism speaks with passion and longing of the happiness to be found in the law of the Lord. Yet for many people—even Christians—the commandments are accepted grudgingly as a necessary but mundane part of the ordered life. To sing of them as sweeter than honey and more precious than gold demands a different approach altogether. This booklet aims to bring about a new appreciation and delight in the law of the Lord—more specifically, in the Ten Commandments.

Most people in Britain are ignorant of the Ten Commandments. If they have heard of them, then they tend see them as a few rather bald prohibitions which are quoted only when it is convenient to do so. The attitude of a young couple discussing their marriage plans on television recently is fairly typical.[1] Although they did not normally go to church, they hoped to have a church wedding because they 'tried to be good.' 'We keep the Ten Commandments,' said the young woman brightly. The man grunted disparagingly, and she responded with an embarrassed laugh, 'Well, not committing adultery, anyway.'

In the wider social and cultural world where the memory of biblical stories and texts is fading, these 'ten words' from God have become distorted in several ways. Where they remain, they are separated from the introduction concerning God's loving care and grace, and left simply as an old-fashioned version of the school rules dictated by a fierce headmaster. Once they are shorn of all context and theology, it is then assumed that obeying them is the only way to please God, the only way to achieve salvation and heaven.

A spot check of a small number of church ministers a couple of years ago[2] indicated that many within the church saw the Commandments as inappropriate and illogical—culturally bound to a millennia-old tradition, *ad hoc* in what they covered, and difficult to handle. In this situation the question is not so much 'What do they demand of me?' but 'How are they relevant to me?' Are they not superseded by the Sermon on the Mount? Is not the law now mercifully buried by the gospel of grace?

---

[1]   From the first programme, *The Soul of Britain*, BBC 2 TV, narrated by Michael Buerk and broadcast in May 2000.

[2]   Reported in the *Today* programme BBC Radio 4, in 1998.

Yet a steady stream of books based on the commandments still comes out. Many of these represent a biblically conservative popular style of writing in which the commandments are used as a vehicle to assess the moral decline of the modern world. This may have some legitimate prophetic force, but there are also dangers. Sometimes social comment dominates and the commandments simply become very small pegs on which to hang pessimistic analysis, losing the context of gracious words to an already-rescued people. Some writing falls into over-simplification where the commandments can end up forming an exclusively personal ethic of 'don't lie,' 'don't steal' and 'be pure.'

This booklet represents a response to such challenges. It brings together an understanding of the context of the Old Testament law with an examination of the individual commandments in the light of their prologue. It goes on to review the commandments in the light of the New Testament teaching, and discuss their place in Christian ethics. Finally, it details some of the possibilities for preaching and teaching the Ten Commandments.

We write in the conviction that—rightly understood—the Ten Commandments are both relevant and life-giving. They are relevant to the young couple 'trying to be good' who associate with the church only for a wedding service. And they are life-giving to those for whom Psalm 119 speaks, who long for the Lord's salvation, whose delight is in his law.

2

'I Brought You Out of Slavery': The Old Testament Context

The Old Testament law is neither simply a 'rule book' nor 'good advice.' It is the gift of God which offers a shape for living, flowing from Israel's covenant relationship with God. Just as Jesus says, 'If you love me, you will obey what I command' (John 14.15) so in the Old Testament: to know God is to follow his law. Obedience is the response of love to the freedom God gives his people (Deut 10.12–13).

The literary setting for the law—*all* of the law from Exodus to Deuteronomy—is that of Mount Sinai.[3] After three months of travelling in the wilderness from Egypt, the people of God set up camp at Sinai. Here God declares his special love for Israel and instructs Moses:

> Thus you shall say to the house of Jacob, and tell the Israelites: You have seen what I did to the Egyptians, and how I bore you on eagles' wings and brought you to myself. Now therefore, if you obey my voice and keep my covenant, you shall be my treasured possession out of all the peoples. Indeed, the whole earth is mine, but you shall be for me a priestly kingdom and a holy nation.
> (Exod 19.3–6)

The people respond with enthusiasm and they prepare themselves to encounter God on the mountain. There God speaks the 'ten words' to the people.[4]

The whole of the law is given in this context, but the Ten Commandments are given first (Exod 20.1–21). In two further ways they are set apart from the rest, as a kind of summary. First, they are the only collection of rules to be repeated in Scripture almost verbatim, in Deut 5.6–21. Second, they are presented as the direct address of God himself to the people. All other laws in the Pentateuch are mediated through Moses—but in Exod 20.1–21 the LORD is speaking to Israel unmediated.

The significance of this direct address of God himself is often missed—most notably by Charlton Heston (as Moses) in the Hollywood version of the story who mediates them loudly to Israel himself! The receiving of the Ten Commandments *from* God involved an encounter *with* God at the same time. Presumably

---

3   There are various law codes in the Pentateuch, which are separated by blocks of narrative. Historians tend to date them to different periods in Israel's history. But according to the narrative they are all ascribed to Moses meeting with God on Sinai, as the normative event according to which Israel establishes its covenant identity.

4   The commandments are referred to as the 'ten words' (thus *Decalogue*, from the Greek) in Exod 34.28, Deut 4.13 and 10.4. *Dabar*, translated 'Commandment' in most versions is more usually translated 'word' or 'deed'; the more usual word for 'commandment' is *mitzvah*.

they thus reveal something characteristic about his nature in the way that no other laws do. Not only are these commandments given personally by God, they are also addressed personally (in the second person singular) to every individual in Israel. This underlines that the law is not something distant. Morality can never be understood in the abstract; it is an aspect of relationship with God. Jesus' parable of the sheep and the goats (Matt 25.31–46) makes a similar point: what is done for others is as done for Christ.

Freedom

The commandments begin with a prologue which is the vital context for a proper understanding of the law. It recurs again and again as a refrain throughout Exodus:

> I am the LORD your God who brought you out of the land of Egypt, out of the house of slavery. (Exod 20.2; *cf* Deut 5.6)

For Jews this statement is so integral to the law that they begin enumerating the commandments right here. This introduction is the first commandment itself.[5]

Prior to any regulations, here is the ultimate statement of the relationship between God and freedom. It provides the basis and the intention for all of the law. *God is giving his people the law because he has freed them and wants them to remain free.* Remember those cruel Egyptian slave-drivers! Do not forget: this freedom from the house of slavery is the reason he asks for a different sort of slavery now.[6] The LORD is the God whose service is perfect freedom.

Christian interpretation has too easily polarized the Old Testament law and the New Testament gospel. In particular, there has been a Protestant tendency to see Judaism as legalistic, which exaggerates the distinction between law and grace. It is clear from the record of the Ten Commandments in Exodus 20 alone how 'gospel' precedes 'law' already in the Old Testament. God's grace is prevenient. God's gift of freedom from Egypt is understood as the rescue from the power of death. Thus to live by these commandments means *life*.

In Matt 19.16, a rich young ruler comes to Jesus and asks what good deed he must do to have eternal life. Jesus replies, 'If you wish to enter into life, keep the commandments.' We trust Jesus meant what he said. These commandments explain the God-given way of living life truly—as their prologue suggests.

This understanding of freedom is very different from that which is popular today. The biblical presentation suggests that freedom is firstly something to be

---

5 There is a long-standing debate as to how to divide up the commandments. We have followed common Protestant practice in the numbering of the Decalogue here, reflecting the paragraph divisions of the Masoretic text of Exodus. Roman Catholic practice has traditionally combined 'You shall have no other gods before me' and 'You shall not make for yourself an idol' to form the first commandment and divided the last commandment on coveting into two, following the Deuteronomic text. The Jewish way considers the prologue as the first, and then combines the two succeeding instructions.

6 The paradox here underlines the two types of slavery: a destructive slavery and a liberating slavery. There is no middle ground.

received and secondly something to be maintained. It is not something that one can gain—but it is something that one can lose. This makes a logical case for the value of boundaries, for the definition of the limits of behaviour, in order that God's freedom be enjoyed and not squandered.

I am the LORD Your God

The prologue begins with God's introduction of himself. There can be no question of who is giving these laws—they are God's direct address to Israel. And whereas 'god' could be understood in a variety of ways (the Hebrew *'el* is a general term): he is *the* LORD, who made himself known by name to Israel when, through Moses, he rescued them from slavery in Egypt (Exod 3.13–15). According to the narrative, this took place just three months previously.

The name 'the LORD' itself reminds Israel of his particular relationship with them. He is 'the LORD *your* God.' All of the commands which follow arise out of this relationship, through which God and Israel promise to live in covenant faithfulness together. The Ten Commandments may be *general* rules but they are not *abstract* rules—as if they were somehow plucked from the sky and imposed on God's people. Rather, they substantiate a particular relationship: they explain how to live with God. And they are given personally *by* God.[7]

Israel has enthusiastically promised to obey God's voice (Exod 19.5) and enter into covenant with God. This covenant is the means by which they will fulfil the promise to Abraham: that, through them, all the families of the earth be blessed. They are excited and expectant, listening out for that voice at Sinai. And here is that voice, explaining to Israel how to keep their side of the agreement. God is speaking personally to Israel—to each individual, in the singular—like a parent to a child, setting out the essential facts of life. This is how they will become a priestly kingdom and a holy nation, bearing God's name and modelling his character so that, through them, all the families of the earth will be blessed (*cf* Gen 12.3).

Written in Stone

These essential facts of life consist of a couple of 'absolute necessities' (keep the Sabbath, honour one's parents) and eight 'absolute limits' ('you shall not…'—those which are negatively formulated). They deal with our attitude to God (especially the first five) and our attitude to neighbour (especially the second five). Yet there is no separation of worship from daily living; we are to honour the living God and we are to look after our ox and ass. The Sabbath command specifically links the attitude to God and neighbour, a link which Jesus reaffirms in his double summary of the law (Matt 22.36–40). Not even a slave is to work on the day which is made holy to God.

---

7   On this point, Hauerwas emphasizes the difference between command (given as personal address) and law (given indirectly). See S Hauerwas, 'The Truth about God: The Decalogue as Condition for Truthful Speech,' *NZSTh* 40 (1998), pp 17–39.

That it is specified how they are written in stone underlines the finality of these 'ten words.' In principle they are valid permanently. The recounting of the Ten Commandments in Deuteronomy—from the settled experience of the promised land—makes clear that it is 'not (just) with our fathers that the LORD made this covenant but with us' (Deut 5.3). And it is specified that, having spoken them out of the fire and cloud, God 'added no more' (Deut 5.22).

The rest of the Old Testament law may be seen as variations on the theme of these Ten Commandments. Their treatment here is suggestive for understanding their role for ethics in general; they provide a full mapping of the boundaries within which life can be well lived. Thus they provide a 'general field' theory of ethics—they offer the foundations, but not all the details. They provide the general principle—which is then to be localized and applied through interpretation.[8]

Consider, for example, the book of Deuteronomy, which applies the Ten Commandments to a new context. Deut 12–13 reflects the first three commandments in the demand for purity of worship and the exclusion of all foreign gods. Deuteronomy 14.28–16.17 improvises upon the fourth commandment, with an emphasis on 'holy rhythms' and care of the poor. Deuteronomy 16.18–18.22 emphasizes the fifth commandment, as the foundation of respect for legitimate human authorities such as judges, kings, priests and prophets. The sixth commandment underlies the opening and closing laws in the section Deut 19.1–21.9, and the eighth, ninth and tenth are alluded to in-between (Deut 19.14–21). Deuteronomy 22.13–30, concerning sexual offences, assumes the seventh commandment. Finally Deut 23–26 assumes the eighth and tenth commandments translated into a community ethos of care and compassion, especially for the weak and poor.

Elsewhere in the Old Testament there are countless stories which illustrate and expound the significance of the Ten Commandments. The prophets chastise Israel precisely for not keeping them, and underline the curses which result. We shall discuss some of these texts as we now consider each of the commandments in turn.

---

8   Though liable to be unsuccessful in practice, it is appropriate *in theory* to understand all of ethics subsumed under the ten commandments (*eg* Calvin).

3
Word by Word

i) You Shall Have No Other Gods Before Me

It is in the nature of God to want an exclusive relationship with his people, the people he has rescued from Egypt. If God is going to enter into covenant with them—through which they will be his treasured possession among all peoples—then the reverse is equally necessary. Thus, living by the covenant involves a choice for God and God alone.

Elsewhere in the Old Testament the analogy is made with marriage.[9] A healthy marriage involves absolute loyalty between the two parties. It is in the nature of the marriage relationship that each partner loves the other 'jealously.' It is in the nature of the LORD that he is a jealous God—he is passionately involved with us. He demands that our relationship with him is exclusive.

Israel learned this lesson the hard way. According to the Exodus narrative, it was not long after receiving the Ten Commandments and completing the covenant, that Israel grew bored in the wilderness. They were tired of waiting for Moses to come down from Mount Sinai. Perhaps, in the desert, the God who had rescued them from Egypt seemed very far away. So they made a golden calf and worshipped it. God's anger was kindled to such an extent that he was ready to destroy the people. But Moses interceded and saved the day. The covenant is re-established, and God reminds Israel of the first commandment (Exod 34.14). It is vital that Israel learn this lesson before arriving in the land of Canaan, where the people will be tempted to go after other gods (Deut 6.10–15).

This first commandment makes loyalty to God the supreme virtue. The references to it elsewhere in the Torah suggest it is also the supreme challenge in a faithless or multi-faith society. The parallel for Western Christians of the twenty-first century, living in a secular and pluralistic society, is precise. We are called to live with absolute allegiance to the God who saves us, whatever the invitations and pressures from competing 'gods.'

The command is not a theological comment on the existence of 'other gods.'[10] It is irrelevant, here, whether or not 'other gods' *actually* exist. This is a practical instruction to look to God for everything in life. Anything which detracts from primary loyalty to the LORD is slavery again.

Following the 'second edition' of the commandments in Deut 5, the first commandment is developed in the following chapter where it is expressed in a positive formulation. This is known to Jews as the *Shema,* and forms the fundamental phrase of their daily prayer:

---

9   Hosea 1–3.
10   The Old Testament addresses this question elsewhere. See, for example, 1 Kings 18.

Hear, O Israel: the LORD is our God, the LORD alone. You shall love the LORD your God with all your heart, and with all your soul, and with all your might.
(Deut 6.4–5)

ii) You Shall Not Make for Yourself an Idol…You Shall Not Bow Down to Them or Worship Them

It follows from the first commandment that we may not worship anything else. The second commandment specifically prohibits the worship of any image of God; this is not worshipping God. The LORD cannot be worshipped in the form of anything in his creation.

The reason for this prohibition is not explained in the Old Testament. The nearest to an explanation is in the re-telling of God's meeting with Israel at Sinai in Deuteronomy:

> Since you saw no form when the LORD spoke to you at Horeb out of the fire, take care and watch yourselves closely, so that you do not act corruptly by making an idol for yourselves, in the form of any figure—the likeness of male or female, the likeness of any animal that is on the earth…(Deut 4.15–18)

Because Israel did not *see* God, but only heard a voice, they are not to make any image of God. Some Christians have taken this to mean that only the *word* matters in worship. Jews have tended to a different extreme, prohibiting all visual representations of God. But the second commandment is not a total iconoclasm; it does not forbid artists from attempting to depict the wonders of God. The very nature of the biblical text itself suggests that this could not be so, given the richness of metaphor, the daring analogies and in particular the extent of the anthropomorphism used for God. Here words are used to create pictures of God—for example as a father, or a shepherd, or a king. Rather, the prohibition is, specifically, about using images of God with a view to worshipping them.

The ultimate theological reason given for this commandment is to be found in Gen 1.26: 'Let us make man in our image, after our likeness.' Perhaps the only acceptable image for God is humanity; human life is the one place in which you can 'see' a representation of God. As Irenaeus put it, 'the glory of God is a human being fully alive.' The incarnation certainly confirms this.

iii) You Shall Not Make Wrongful Use of the Name of the LORD Your God

The Israelites and now (by adoption) Christians are those who are privileged to have been given God's name. This represents God's total investment of himself and his character in his people; these people are his witnesses. His name is given at the point where God calls Moses to lead the people out of slavery in Egypt (Exod 3.13–14).

To know God's name, by this great revelation from God, requires that we rightly use the name. In other words, how we live for God (ethics) cannot be separated from the way we talk about God (theology). Because we know God's name, we cannot make God mean anything we want. That would be denying God's name, which is at the heart of the concern here.

The original context of this commandment refers primarily to the use of the name in swearing oaths, typically in the form 'as the LORD lives' (thus, *cf* James 5.12; Matt 5.37). In modern parlance 'swearing' has come to be understood in a more casual sense. But these commandments are addressed to believers, to those who claim to know God and worship him—not to non-believers who might be prone to use his name casually because it bears little meaning. The third commandment is not simply about profanity. The Hebrew of 'in vain' means insincerely, as expressed more graphically in Psalm 24.3–4.

Another term for blasphemy is lying, and clearly this is most serious when it is done in the guise of God's name. The false prophets described in the Old Testament are classic examples of this. They attempt to manipulate people by speaking with the apparent authority of divine sanction when, in fact, they have no authority but their own misleading voice and they know it.

The implication is clear. The third commandment pinpoints the human tendency to justify a position or a programme by appealing to 'what God really wants.' It highlights the most serious of all attempts to manipulate people—by using God's name in vain.

God's people, who bear God's name and thus embody his character in the world, are not to misrepresent God. The command is highly relevant to Christians engaged in evangelism. Both the form and content of the witness must be absolutely true to the God who has revealed himself in Christ. No exaggeration; no half-truths. In word and action God's people are to be wary of misrepresenting him, of taking his name in vain, of 'forgetting' the One who has been given the name that is above all other names (Phil 2.9).

iv) Remember the Sabbath Day

For Jews, this commandment carries central importance. It has been said, 'It is not just the Jews that kept the Sabbath, but the Sabbath that kept the Jews.' The keeping of Sabbath has become for them a distinctive mark of identity down the centuries.

The reason given for remembering the Sabbath is different in the two accounts of the Ten Commandments. In Exodus the principle is based on the work of the LORD in creation (Exod 20.11), and in Deuteronomy it is the gift of redemption from Egypt which is the reason for obedience (Deut 5.15). The fundamental principle is the same in both texts, however, and is evident throughout Scripture: the imitation of God. God is our fundamental model for behaviour. There is a pattern to God's work that makes it appropriate for us too—to rest one day in seven.[11]

Exodus 31.12–17 explains why this is so important:

---

11 For more on this, see A J Heschel, *The Sabbath: Its Meaning for Modern Man* (New York: Farrar, Straus and Giroux, 1951).

You shall keep my Sabbaths, for this is a sign between me and you throughout your generations, given in order that you may know that I, the LORD, sanctify you…Therefore the Israelites shall keep the Sabbath, observing the Sabbath throughout their generations, as a perpetual covenant…

Through the work of creation and redemption, God has *sanctified* Israel—he has made them holy. So the people are to keep a day of holiness, a day for remembering the covenant by which they themselves belong to the LORD. The giving of one day to the LORD and keeping it holy is a symbol of the whole of life, which is given to the LORD. As with the giving of money, the giving of a portion symbolizes how the *whole* belongs to God.

Remembering the Sabbath involves desisting from all work—all people, including visitors and slaves, and even all animals. Exodus 16.22–30 indicates that God will specially provide for Israel, in order that they do not need to work on the seventh day. This stresses that the command to rest is not a luxury just for the well-off, but a rest for all alike. There is a principle of justice involved here. Those who are at risk, in need and on the margins should thus be protected from the pressure to overwork. The corporate experience of working together and resting together is also important.

There is great debate in the gospels on the subject of Sabbath observance. Its purpose had become distorted, such that it had turned into a day of petty restrictions and burdensome legislation. So Jesus underlines that 'the Sabbath was made for humankind, and not humankind for the Sabbath' (Mark 2.27). He challenges the Pharisees who had 'lost the plot'; they were keeping the commandment in the wrong way for the wrong reasons. The Sabbath is not a matter for Jewish national pride. Rather, it is God's gift at creation. Thus Israel neither owns it nor controls it. Moreover, it is designed to enrich life and make it better, a reminder of all God's gifts—not something to burden life.

The Sabbath commandment focuses some important issues for a Christian response to Israelite law. More specifically, it highlights the need to distinguish between what is general, in application, and what is particular. This is the subject of the next chapter. While recognizing the universal and everlasting character of the Ten Commandments, Christian tradition has moved Sabbath observance from Saturday to Sunday—the day of resurrection, the day of God's new creation. Aside from gathering as the church to worship, the practices of desisting from work and marking it as holy are varied. In an age of increased Sunday trading, the challenge lies in retaining some distinct features of this day. The purpose of this is to enable a weekly rhythm of work and rest which is shared—by rich and poor alike—and an opportunity for acknowledging God's grace and blessing in all things.

v) Honour Your Father and Mother

On the assumption that all of the commandments are addressed to adults in Israel, then this command is primarily concerned with how adults treat their parents. Though legitimate, it is thus an extension of the text to apply it to children. To 'honour' is to give esteem and respect. Sometimes a stronger word is used, meaning fear or reverence (*eg* Lev 19.3); but the command does not specify any particular actions, nor obedience.

Ruth is noteworthy for such regard and concern. She expresses total loyalty— 'where you go I will go…where you die I will die' (Ruth 1.16–17)—and this not to her mother but her mother-in-law. Elsewhere the Old Testament is not uncritical of parents or unaware of the complicating issues which may arise in the relationship. David, for example, is presented consistently as a poor father: he spoils Absalom, and misery results (2 Sam 13.21; 2 Sam 15.6). The relationship of Jonathan to Saul is another complicated one. On the one hand, Jonathan is loyal to his father even to death; yet, in the end, he is forced to maintain his own integrity at the expense of loyalty to his father.

In the gospels, Jesus talks about the need to 'hate' one's parents (Luke 14.26) in order to be a disciple. This is a strong way of saying that there are loyalties greater than to parents. Obeying the fifth commandment may involve a critical obedience. If it conflicts with obedience to God, then disobedience may be appropriate. This suggests that the structuring of the Ten Commandments is significant: the first commandment takes priority.

The outcome of this command is 'that your days may be long in the land that the LORD your God is giving you.' This is neither strictly a promise (*cf* Eph 6.2) nor a reward. Rather, it is an intrinsic consequence for the community, *ie* when all people fulfil their social obligations. The commandments are given to create a society which is holy, characterized by peace and grace, thus reflecting God's name and nature. Therefore, the case of a rebellious son is very serious for the people as a whole (Deut 21.18–21).

vi) You Shall Not Murder

Because this command is expressed in just one Hebrew word—*rasah*—it is vital to examine the precise meaning and extent of the term. It is variously translated as 'murder' and 'kill.' Yet in certain circumstances the Old Testament permits the taking of life, thus the meaning of this commandment is determined by the context.

There are five Hebrew words which are used for the taking of life. Three refer to the taking of life in the context of war. A fourth applies to legal penalties, where it is determined that a person deserves to die. Only the fifth, *rasah*, is prohibited. Normally, it refers to murder, as with Ahab and Jezebel murdering Naboth (1 Kings 21.19). However, it is not only used of premeditated murder. It can also refer to unintentional manslaughter (*eg* in the regulations concerning cities of refuge, Num 35.9–34 and Deut 4.41–42). Nevertheless, 'murder' is probably closer to its overall meaning than 'kill.'

The basis of the command is that all life belongs to God (Lev 17.11; Gen 9.6). The divine intention in creation is that no life be taken. Life is thus not for human beings to do with as they will. It is up to God to determine what shall be done with life. The issue thus becomes one of discernment regarding that divine will. Human beings are never to kill on their own authority; they are only agents of God.

Israel's limited use of capital punishment, as specified in certain God-given laws (see Exod 21.12–17; 22.18–20), had to do with violations of God's created order. Similar arguments were used regarding fighting and war; indeed, death is the penalty for disobeying most of the Ten Commandments. The issue for discernment is the matter of how to restore God's world under God's authority. This remains the central issue in wrestling with matters of war, capital punishment, self-defence, suicide, euthanasia and abortion today.

Yet the matter of taking life is not the most serious concern in the Old or New Testaments. Debasement or corruption, for example, are more serious than death. In Jesus' own reference to the sixth commandment (Matt 5.21–26), he intensifies it—in particular contexts—to include verbal abuse and other manifestations of anger and power. Above all, he asserts that reconciliation among those estranged from one another be given a high priority, even above religious practice.

vii) You Shall Not Commit Adultery

This commandment addresses the place of the family and the need for loyalty. The integrity of marriage is at the very centre of Israelite society—it is not merely a private matter. The violation of this loyalty through adultery is so serious that the death penalty is prescribed (see Deut 22.22), even for a king (2 Sam 12.13).

Adultery is not only a crime against another person or persons. It is also a sin against God himself (Gen 39.9; 2 Sam 12.9). It violates God's intention at creation, according to which man and woman leave their parents and become one flesh (Gen 2.24). Furthermore, as with the breaking of any of the commandments, it challenges directly the covenant relationship with God. The breaking of the covenant with God by turning to other 'gods' is called adultery.

The term is used with both men and women as the subject of the verb. It concerns those who are married and those who are betrothed or engaged (see Lev 18.6–20; 20.10–21; Deut 22.23–29). There is, however, a difference in the way it bears on women and men. A woman commits adultery against her own marriage whether or not the other man she partners is married, whereas a man only commits adultery with another married woman. Thus the man commits a sin against the other man, but the woman commits a sin against her husband. This reflects the patriarchal character of Israel. Jesus puts men and women on an equal footing with respect to this commandment (Matt 5.27, 32).

The story of David's adultery with Bathsheba (2 Sam 11) emphasizes the social implications of the commandment. The actual act of adultery is only a part of the problem. A web of chaos results which affects countless people, not merely Bathsheba and her husband Uriah. After this episode, the first problem in David's own household is that of adultery between Amnon and Tamar. David fails to act because of his own lack of integrity. He becomes angry but he has lost the authority with which to speak out (2 Sam 13.21).

This commandment is addressed to all people, whether married or not. It places a social responsibility on every member of the community to respect the marriage commitment, and work always to support those relationships.

viii) You Shall Not Steal

As with all of the commandments, the problem with stealing is that it breaks relationships. It is a sin against the neighbour, which is much more serious than a property crime. The penalty for stealing (explained in the more detailed laws) is usually some form of restitution (*eg* Exod 22), not death as in the previous commandments. Its effects can be dealt with socially and economically.

It is a common mistake to appeal to this commandment in defence of property rights. Though it assumes private- (or family-) owned property, it does not justify it. This is about maintaining justice and not the *status quo*. Thus, by extension, the command is a warning to those who have plenty just as much as it is a warning to those who have little. The rich may be guilty of some kind of 'legalized' theft, which is the cause of poverty. Theft may be anything which undermines justice, including the wrong use of power. This is exemplified by Jezebel in taking over Naboth's vineyard (1 Kings 21). Legalized theft is theft nonetheless.

Some of the detailed laws that follow the Ten Commandments give us a glimpse of the full import of this command. It is translated into a community ethic of care and generosity, especially for the poor and the weak (Lev 25.37; Deut 24.6, 14), often enshrined in agricultural terms. So landowners must not harvest to the edges of their fields, so that the poor may glean some food (Lev 19.9f).

The thrust of the command about stealing is not to make sure no one steals from me. Like the rich young ruler it is possible to say, 'I have not stolen. I have kept this commandment' (*cf* Mark 10.17–22). But the implication of Jesus' reply is that not stealing involves far more than simply not taking things that belong to someone else.

The rich young ruler needed to give away his possessions to find righteousness—which suggest, perhaps, he was guilty of stealing in a wider social sense. His situation raises poignant issues for an affluent society. The attachment to material things, the extravagance of many lifestyles and the mountains of waste generated—all in the face of widespread hunger and need—raise the question of theft to new levels. The prophets rail against Israel concerning precisely these things (Is 3.16–26; Amos 8.4–6; Micah 2.1–3; *cf* James 5.1–6).

ix) You Shall Not Bear False Witness Against Your Neighbour

This is primarily concerned with bearing witness in a court of law. The problem is the same as that described more fully in Deut 19.15–21, for which the penalty is severe:

> A single witness shall not suffice to convict a person of any crime…only on the evidence of two or three witnesses shall a charge be sustained…If the witness is a false witness, having testified falsely against another, then you shall do to the false witness just as the false witness had meant to do to the other.

This is not the restriction of an irritable judge. In a canonical context, it is the direction of God to a people who, three months out of Egypt, need to learn how to live as a *people* again. As with the previous eight commandments, God is providing the means for the people to be free, and to rebuild the structures of worship, work, family and justice. Any injustice and false testimony against a neighbour is against another child of the covenant, and therefore against God himself.

This commandment condemns lying on the basis that (in general) it undermines the justice system and (in particular) it hurts a fellow Israelite. The case of Naboth's vineyard is a prime example of false witness in court (1 Kings 21). Jezebel arranges, in King Ahab's name, for two false witnesses to bring a charge against Naboth—for which he is stoned. The scenario apparently complies with the law in Deut 19 yet it also demonstrates its abuse. Similarly, abuse is sanctioned in the trial of Jesus. Both Matthew and Mark are explicit that false witnesses are procured in order to produce the wanted outcome (Matt 26.59–61; Mark 14.55–59).

This commandment attributes great importance to the tongue. That which is voiced—especially with the force of the law or the authority of a king behind it—carries great weight and is not to be taken lightly. The seriousness of the spoken word is underlined in the wisdom books, especially Psalms and Proverbs, also in Matthew and James (Matt 12.33–37; *cf* 5.33–37; James 3.1–12). The scope of the command includes slander (Deut 5.20; Matt 15.19), but the reference is not merely to trivial gossip. Fundamentally, it is that the way you speak that reflects the person you are.

x) You Shall Not Covet

Unlike all the other commandments, the emphasis here is on one's inner intentions—rather than outward actions. The Hebrew term for 'covet' is not necessarily a negative word. It is used, for example, of the mountain which God *desires* in Ps 68.7. It is the context which makes the desire unlawful as with David coveting Bathsheba or Ahab coveting Naboth's vineyard. It addresses the attitudes of the heart or mind that lead to wrongful action. Without covetousness, disobedience to the other commandments would probably not occur.

Arguably this is the most demanding commandment. True obedience involves avoiding not only certain actions but also intentions or attitudes towards others such as envy or greed or lust. Jesus stresses this in the Sermon on the Mount (Matt 5.21–22, 27–28), drawing out the coveting roots of all disobedience.

Covetousness betrays a dissatisfaction with what I have. It suggests that I am unable to distinguish between what I need and what I desire. It always feeds a hunger for more, which inevitably leads to social and economic friction.

There is a sense in which the tenth commandment brings one back to the first. If the first commandment is followed, then the tenth—and thus all the rest—are unlikely to present problems. This brings us to the New Testament context, where Jesus and Paul underline the same sentiment (*cf* Col 3.1–5).

4
Superseded or Redefined?
The New Testament Context

This chapter can only provide a brief outline and some examples of the treatment of the Commandments in the New Testament. The many references to 'the Law' include them although the scope of the word 'Law' varies, sometimes probably referring to the Decalogue on its own, sometimes to the Pentateuch and sometimes to the whole of the Hebrew Scriptures.

The handling of the Ten Commandments in the New Testament involves the much bigger issue of the status and practice of the law after the coming of Christ, and the continuities and discontinuities between the two testaments. This issue is raised throughout the text from Jesus' clashes with the religious authorities, through Peter's vision of clean and unclean animals, to Paul's grappling with the tensions between Gentile and Jewish believers. As we have shown in chapter 2, these 'ten words,' repeated twice and given directly by God, written in stone, are given a greater weight than the rest of the commands and precepts of the Pentateuch. But do they retain their status and significance in the New Testament? And if so, in what way?

The commandments are quoted, particularly those about social relationships, in a variety of contexts. By looking at several of the texts where they are quoted, we can see the wider teaching involved; teaching on discipleship and ethics, on judgment, law and sin; on the danger of making obedience to the detail of the law the focus of discipleship; on the meaning of freedom from the law in the life of the Spirit.

The Commandments in the Gospels

The gospel writers record several different ways in which Jesus handles the Ten Commandments. In the Sermon on the Mount, in Matthew 5 for example, he sets out his teaching about the radical nature of discipleship, and in verses 17 to 20 outlines his relationship to the law. This is not an easy passage, but one that needs to be grappled with if we wish to understand the role of the law in the Christian life. The 'Do not think…' of verse 17, suggests that many did think that Jesus had set out to abolish the law, since he had challenged the authorities on both Sabbath keeping, and ritual cleanliness. The emphasis seems to be that Jesus fulfils, a word carrying a range of meanings, the whole of the Old Testament, the law and the prophets. The obedient Christian will be guided by the Old Testament in a range of ways, but will not exhibit the legalism of the teachers of the law.

Jesus then goes on to explain by several examples, some drawn from the Ten Commandments, how this works out in practice, ending in verse 48 with a summary that pulls together all the commandments from one to ten.

The rich young man who appears in Matthew 19, and in Mark and Luke, questions Jesus, whose answers imply that discipleship involves more than obeying the law; that only God is good, and even our good deeds do not make us good; that the commandments are pointers to God's goodness; that, as in Matthew 5.48, the call is to be perfect, so even though he may sincerely claim to have kept them, he still lacks something in his discipleship. At the least, Jesus' answer (that he should sell his possessions and give to the poor) suggests that being a disciple involves radical interpreting of the commandments.

Jesus sums up the law in the two commandments, love God and love your neighbour, from Deuteronomy 6.4–5 and Leviticus 19.18. (Mark 12.29-31 and parallels). He does this in answer to a testing question on the greatest commandment. He also receives these two as a response to a question he asks in Luke 10. Here again he responds to the question about the neighbour with a story that drove the meaning of neighbour beyond kin, community and friendly alien, to 'those who hate you.'

He challenges the keepers of the law over a number of issues including Sabbath observance, and (in Matthew 15) over honouring parents, again showing that radical discipleship means understanding the law in the light of love for God and neighbour. God's rescue and redemption require a covenant commitment to an obedience which is true to the nature of God, and which does not lose sight of the central position—I am the LORD your God who brought you out...love the LORD your God.

The Commandments and Paul

The tension in Paul, as in the gospels, is between two meanings of the fulfilment of the law. Echoing Matthew 5 in certain respects, there are radical statements about abolition and conservative ones about continuing validity side by side in different forms. Out of all the writing that deals with the issues of Christian living and the role of the law, the working out of law and grace, works and justification, rule-based and Spirit-based life, we have space to look at two, Galatians and particularly part of chapter 5, and Romans 13.8–10.

In Galatians it is helpful to distinguish between the social function of the law and its moral function. Socially the law defined the demarcation line between Jews and Gentiles. Either Gentile converts to Christianity had to take on the law, or the barrier of the law between the two groups of believers was gone. Jesus has broken down the barrier, the law is fulfilled, the social function of the law has ended.

The moral function of the law, especially the Ten Commandments as the primary statement of the law, is in a different category. We do not earn God's blessing by keeping the law, but the keeping of the law and the commandments is the appropriate response to God's blessing. This is, of course, what God is saying in the Ten Commandments. But some commentators go further and point to Galatians 5.1–6 where Paul proclaims freedom from obligation to the Mosaic law, and ends with another summary based on relationships with God and with others. 'The only thing that counts is faith working through love.' Here some would argue that 'Paul proclaims freedom from obligation to the Mosaic law not only as the basis for beginning the Christian life but also as the basis for continuing the Christian life.'[12]

It is important to remember that Paul's apparently negative statements about the law came in response to two groups of people: either (a) Jews who rejected Jesus and thereby continued to depend upon the law to maintain their relationship with God, or (b) those who insisted that one had to keep the law's demands in order to become a Christian. In both cases, what was good but temporary (the law) effectively became the enemy of what was best and lasting (Christ, the fulfilment of the law). Like all other Jews Paul saw the law as a gift from God, a good and holy thing (Rom 7); the problem was that now in the light of Christ, its function had changed.

The law has a negative moral function in that it exposes sin, making it named and known. However, by itself the law lacks the power to effect the moral transformation that it requires. 'Now if the ministry that brought death, which was engraved in letters on stone, came with glory, will not the ministry of the Spirit be even more glorious?' (2 Cor 3.7) What the law cannot do God does by grace; Jesus delivers Christians from the law's demands, 'having cancelled the written code with its regulations, nailing it to the cross' (Col 2.13) and removing the curse and supervision of the law. The Spirit reproduces his righteousness in us so that we live in the power of the Spirit for God by serving one another in love, thus fulfilling the commandments. Galatians 5.13 and 14 sum the law up again, but begin 'Do not use your freedom to indulge the sinful nature.'

Romans 13.8–10 again contains the summary, 'Love your neighbour as yourself. Love does no harm to its neighbour. Therefore love is the fulfilment of the law.' The commands that Paul lists—no murder, no adultery, no stealing, no coveting—can never be 'done,' in the sense of reaching the end of our obligations, because there is a continuing debt to love one another. The commitment is lifelong. 'Clothe yourselves with the Lord Jesus Christ, and do not think about how to gratify the desires of the sinful nature.' Has the Spirit sufficient power to produce this moral living if the foundations of the law are not reemphasized? In Paul's own day his position worried those who considered that it would encourage sin. He is aware of this and grapples with the issue in Romans 6, for example.

Has the law's curse been removed, though its precepts must still be followed? Does the moral law still stand, though the ritual law has been done away with? It is not easy to draw the distinction between ritual laws and laws relating to the very specific social, political and economic conditions of the time, and the moral laws that can have universal validity. The Ten Commandments have aspects of all these. All the law has relevance and is necessary for the understanding of the

---

12 G W Hansen, *Galatians* (IVP/US, 1994) p 27; see also S Westerholm, *Israel's Law and the Church's Faith* (Eerdmans, 1988) ch 10, 'The Law and Christian Behaviour.'

mission and ministry of Jesus, the church as the people of God, the nature of the covenant committed life, and the moral demands of Spirit-empowered discipleship. The law still acts as guide, a warning and a definition of the outer parameters of moral action.

It is usually the last six commandments that are being dealt with in the above examples. Texts on the Sabbath are most common in the gospels, but Colossians 2.16 also mentions the Sabbath day, suggesting that how it is kept is a matter of personal or church conscience. Regarding idols and idolatry, 'We know that an idol is nothing at all' says Paul, (1 Cor 8.4), but goes on to work out how Christians should deal with the idolatry around them and eating food given to idols. A wider definition of idolatry is used in Col 3.5 and Eph 5.5. 'In my name,' is a phrase often used by Jesus himself, and all the letter writers—James 5.14, Romans 10.13, Hebrews 1.4, 1 John 5.13—give Jesus the name that is above all names, at whose name every knee should bow.

The apostle Peter tells the churches of mixed Gentile and Jewish descent that *they* are the chosen people, the royal priesthood, a holy nation, a people belonging to God (1 Peter 2.9). He echoes the great promises of Exodus 19.5 and 6. But the new covenant, the conferring of these great titles on small Christian fellowships carries the obligation to model God's character as a holy nation and to mediate as a royal priesthood, his mercy, love and judgment to the rest of the world. Yes, of course, the commandments should be obeyed, but not because they in themselves are the foundation of the life of faith in Christ, but because they will be subsumed in the Spirit-filled life of love.

5
'Do Not Forget':
Teaching the Ten Commandments

Any teaching of the Ten Commandments should give sufficient weight to the context, both from the Old and New Testaments. It is possible to teach them so that they lead to ethical and moral discussion of the good life, but provide no challenge to those who do not love the Lord, nor remind those who do of the solemn commitment embodied in the covenant. They cannot simply be presented as a list of rules to keep, in or out of the kingdom.

The context of the covenant made by the Lord and the people, after they had been miraculously rescued, is enormously important for the whole salvation story and needs to be reiterated before each and every separate commandment. The importance of the covenant commitment, undertaken by the people in community as well as each individual, responsible to God and to each other before God needs stressing. But Christians today need to have in mind as well the summing up of the law by Jesus in the two great commandments, and some idea of what it means to have the glorious freedom of the children of God, dead to the law because they are alive in the Spirit.

Possible Structures of a Programme
Some of these may seem obvious, but programmes can sometimes change the way we handle material. Working out aims and objectives, deciding what needs emphasizing and what kinds of discussion would benefit those taking part, will influence the approach.
• working through the commandments one by one;
• grouping the first four and then the last six;
• teaching from Exodus, with the first session looking at chapter 19;
• teaching them from Deuteronomy and illustrating from the rest of the book, using Deut 10.12–22, as the summarizing covenant passage;
• beginning each talk with a story from Scripture that illustrates each commandment;
• beginning with 21st century stories to illustrate (but not all stories of failure!);
• working backwards so that the programme culminates with 'no other gods;'
• basing the series on the two great commandments, including the ten under each;
• combining the OT reading with a NT reading.

Ways of Teaching
It is useful to know whether those being taught know the Ten Commandments; an anonymous 'test' quickly done so that nothing can be looked up, would

provide a starting point. Asking for the six things you would tell your children not to do can produce an interesting comparison.

If the treatment of the commandments involves discussion about their meaning for moral living today as a Christian, then methods of interactive learning, feed-back, questions and group work, would help the teacher to know how current thinking on social and ethical issues is shaped, and to respond in the most helpful way. When discussion gets on to some of the outworkings of the commandments, Christians do disagree. Of course, everyone agrees that stealing is wrong, but looking at some of the texts from Deuteronomy involving justice and fair economic treatment can raise issues where there is disagreement. Discussion on the Jubilee 2000 debt cancellation programme may be pushing 'Do not steal' rather far, but it is a current topic in this kind of forum.

Aims and Objectives
i) Building up the Church as the Body of Christ

The church is now the recipient of the covenant promises, with the obligation to obey her Lord, and be a holy people, a mediating priesthood, a model of God's character to the world. Because the commandments speak of individual responsibility in community, the flip side of the commandments is that we must not make it difficult for our neighbours in the fellowship, or in the community as a whole, to obey them. The church should be encouraging goodness! The application of the commandments to community life, as well as to individuals, should be an on-going process, involving teaching, praying and discussing ways forward in the light of what has been learnt.

ii) Helping Christians to Learn to Use the Whole Bible, Rather than Focus on a Particular Passage Without Referring to Other Parts of the Text

The commandments have frequently been handled as if they stand on their own. They too need to be taught in the context of the whole of Scripture. Because the Bible weaves narrative and law together, as well all the other literary forms in the Old Testament, then we should be encouraged to use different styles and approaches. The implication of the narrative form throughout Scripture is that there is a process, within the framework of the commandments as set out in Exodus and Deuteronomy, of working out their meaning for different times and circumstances. We can read the stories of failure and repeated forgiveness, stories showing how the curses do take effect, with still the possibility of return and renewal of the blessings. We have given a number of examples in chapter three—Naboth's vineyard, David and Bathsheba, David and his children, Saul and Jonathan, Ruth, Orpah and Naomi, Jesus and his mother and siblings in the gospels, the making of the golden calf—and there are, of course, many others. The prophets and their lists of Israel's failings, involving idolatry and social and economic injustice can also be woven in.

iii) Giving an Introduction to Christian Ethics

Just as the Ten Commandments are addressed to those who have been rescued by God and in freedom are committed to serve him, so Christian ethics
involve reflection on issues of morality, good and bad, right and wrong in the
context of Christian commitment and discipleship. This is far too big a topic to
cover here, but obviously the Ten Commandments frequently play a significant
part in courses on Christian biblical ethics. The use of the Bible in Christian ethics
has varied enormously, with the emphases on the ethical role of story, the forma-
tion of character and the fruits of the Spirit, as well as on rule-based and conse-
quence-based systems.

Based on the two great commandments given by Jesus and the example of his
life and ministry, Christians need to work out how to live, what is right and wrong,
using the Ten Commandments as part of the resources of Scripture. Injunctions
such as, 'Do not commit adultery,' are the outer boundaries of a far richer ethic of
marriage, which might include the Song of Songs, the early chapters of Genesis,
the household codes of the New Testament, and above all the metaphors of marriage used to describe the Lord's relationship with us, which provide an ideal
with implications that take a lifetime to work out and which go far beyond the
simple but uniquely important requirement that we should not commit adultery.

The place of rules in ethics is an area of considerable argument and to illustrate this, it is interesting to consider the influence of situation ethics and the rule
of love. Fletcher's book, *Situation Ethics*[13] had a great deal of influence on subse-
quent Christian ethics. He takes an extreme position and argues that love is the
only Christian norm, and that although moral rules are useful guides, in the end
love and love alone must discern what is the loving thing to do. Although this
book is old and most ordinary Christians have not read it, this view is often voiced
in everyday discussions of what it means to be ethical. It is a popular view that as
long as you love, then you will know how to act for the good. Therefore the need
to argue for the importance of rules, and particularly for the Ten Commandments,
to provide the outer parameters beyond which we cannot go, is very important.
Love in the hands and hearts of fallen humans is, like everything else, a very
fallible guide to moral behaviour.

---

13   J Fletcher, *Situation Ethics* (1966).

6
Resources

Hauerwas, S and Willimon, W H, *The Truth about God: The Ten Commandments in Christian Life* (Nashville: Abingdon Press, 1999)

Segal, B-Z (ed), *The Ten Commandments in History and Tradition* (Jerusalem: Magnes Press, 1992)

Janzen, W, *Old Testament Ethics: A Paradigmatic Approach* (Louisville: Westminster/John Knox, 1994)

Brooks, R, *The Spirit of the Ten Commandments: Shattering the Myth of Rabbinic Legalism* (San Francisco: Harper and Row, 1990)

Commentaries
Larsson, G, *Bound for Freedom: The Book of Exodus in Jewish and Christian Traditions* (Hendrickson, 1999)

Childs, B S, *The Book of Exodus* (Old Testament Library; London: SCM, 1974)

Fretheim, T E, *Exodus* (Interpretation; Louisville: John Knox, 1991)

Miller, P D, *Deuteronomy* (Interpretation; Louisville: John Knox, 1990)

Wright, C, *Deuteronomy* (New International Biblical Commentary; Paternoster, 1996)

More Popular Books
John, J, *God's Top Ten: Rediscovering the Basic Building Blocks for Life* (Kingsway, 1995)

Field, D, *God's Good Life: The Ten Commandments for the Twenty-first Century* (IVP, 1992)

Edwards, B H, *The Ten Commandments for Today* (Day One Publications, 1996)

Warner, R, *The Ten Commandments and the Decline of the West* (Kingsway 1997)

Multi-media
The Ten Commandments (Cecil B DeMille ; US 1923 and US, Paramount 1956). DeMille's first version includes a 'modern' story, with a moral, about two sons of a church-going mother. The second has Charlton Heston striding around as Moses, and Yul Brynner being Pharaoh. Three-and-a-half hours long, the spectacular just begins to overwhelm. However, extracts from the video would liven up Sunday evening sermons.

Moses (Gianfranco De Bosio; UK/Italy 1975). An earnest but superficial attempt to tell the story of Moses. The photography is great and Burt Lancaster is not too bad as Moses.

Testament, is a series of nine titles animating Old Testament stories, including a brooding and dramatic version of the Exodus, made by Russian animators and produced by S4C. They are available from the Bible Society and from Christian bookshops.

Art
The artist Paul Hobbs is currently producing a large interactive piece of work consisting of actual building blocks containing the words of the ten commandments and illustrations pertaining to them. It is designed for exploring their foundational nature and making contemporary application. Contact: arthobbs@globalnet.co.uk